D1302183

Life-Giving Prayer

Practical Ways to Improve Your
Communication with God

Deborah Perkins

Copyright © 2017 Deborah Perkins

Publisher: His Inscriptions, Inc., 2 Hastings Avenue, Worcester, MA 01606

All rights reserved. This book or any portion thereof
may not be reproduced or used in any manner whatsoever
without the express written permission of the publisher
except for the use of brief quotations in a book review.

**Scripture quotations taken from the New American Standard
Bible® (NASB), Copyright © 1960, 1962, 1963, 1968, 1971, 1972, 1973,
1975, 1977, 1995 by The Lockman Foundation
Used by permission. www.Lockman.org.**

Scripture taken from the Holy Bible, NEW INTERNATIONAL VERSION®,
NIV® Copyright © 1973, 1978, 1984, 2011 by Biblica, Inc.® Used by permission.
All rights reserved worldwide.

Scripture taken from the New King James Version. Copyright © 1982 by Thomas
Nelson, Inc. Used by permission. All rights reserved.

Scripture quotations from The ESV® Bible (The Holy Bible, English Standard
Version®), copyright © 2001 by Crossway, a publishing ministry of Good
News Publishers. Used by permission. All rights reserved.

Cover Photo by: Carli Jeen on Unsplash

DEDICATION

Dedicated to the faithful readers of His Inscriptions,

and to the Lord Jesus Christ, the original Author.

CONTENTS

INTRODUCTION

A leading Christian organization, Barna Research group, has determined that prayer is – and has been for decades – the most common spiritual practice among Americans.[1]

No matter what denomination, people of faith are people of prayer, believing in a God who defies the barriers of time and distance to come to the aid of His people.

I, too, have seen the power of prayer, both personally and corporately. But I have also seen that most believers pray alone, not together, and often wonder whether their prayers are making any difference.

This book was birthed out of my desire to mentor and disciple those who long to connect with God more intimately. Wouldn't it be wonderful, I thought, to open the windows into that great mystery we call prayer, and to talk about our experiences communicating with God in ways that become life-giving to others as well? It is my hope that this book you hold in your hands will inspire you to discover Life-Giving Prayer with a God who loves you immensely and desires above all things to build relationship with you.

Deborah Perkins

[1] Roxanne Stone, Editor in chief, Barna research Group, as cited in "Silent and Solo: How Americans Pray;" Barna Research Releases in Faith and Christianity, August 15, 2017).

DEBORAH PERKINS

1
IS THAT YOU, GOD?

A well-known Christian teacher posted an interesting question on Facebook once. He asked: "What is your #1 question or concern about hearing God's voice?"

He received nearly 200 responses to his question. Not surprisingly, the majority of them had to do with distinguishing God's voice from the devil's - or their own.

Just for fun, I asked my children what *their* #1 question was. My two older children said the same thing: "How do I know if it's God speaking?"

However, my youngest, who does hear from God occasionally, has come up with a solution to this problem. As I took a long walk with this adorable one, he explained how prayer works for him. He knows that God wants us to put others' interests above our own (Philippians 2:3), so he has decided that when he hears several voices in his head, he'll choose the *second* one, since Satan (in his pride) probably wants to speak first!

Certain religious traditions have oversimplified the process of hearing God, teaching what I call the "Stoplight Approach." Afraid of encouraging people to "imagine" what God might be saying, they teach instead that God has only three possible answers to our prayers: "Yes," "No," and "Wait."

Ouch.

One look at the elaborate prophecies in scripture, along with the eloquent discourses of our Savior, is enough to convince me that God is by no means limited to a three-word vocabulary!

But how do we overcome our fear of hearing Him? And how do we discern His voice, if He really is speaking? Thankfully, we are not limited to childish conjecture when it comes to hearing God. I believe there is a better - and biblical - way.

A Better Way: Three Steps to Discerning the Voice of God

1. Draw Close

"Draw near to God and He will draw near to you" (James 4:8, NKJV).

There are two types of proximity: physical and emotional/ spiritual. In a crowded room, I can pull up a chair and sit near you in order to hear what you are saying; this physical proximity is a necessary requirement for hearing. The closer we are to someone, the more we hear. We draw near to God in this way by spending regular time in the Word, which is the starting point for all of His communication with us.

The second type of proximity is emotional or, in the case of prayer, spiritual. Growing intimacy with someone gives us access to a broader range of communication because of a heart-to-heart, trusting relationship. As we know someone better, we can almost anticipate what they might say or do in a certain situation. Similarly, as we spend time getting to know God and sharing our hearts with Him, He reveals more of His heart to us. Communication expands far beyond "Yes, No, and Wait," becoming deeper and far more meaningful.

The best way to discern God's voice is to be intimately familiar with the real thing. Just as a bank teller is trained to recognize a counterfeit by handling hundreds of real bills first, so we need to train ourselves to recognize truth when we hear it. As we read in 2 Timothy 3:16-17, the Word of God is our measuring stick:

> *All scripture is given by inspiration of God,*
> *and is profitable for doctrine, for reproof,*
> *for correction, for instruction in righteousness,*
> *that the man of God may be complete,*
> *thoroughly equipped for every good work.*
> *(2 Timothy 3:16-17 NKJV)*

2. Seek Counsel.

Jesus's sheep will "by no means follow a stranger, but will flee from him, because they do not know the voice of a stranger." (John 10:5)

There is safety in numbers, especially for sheep, and it is no accident that Christ uses the analogy of sheep with a shepherd to describe believers like us. The predators -

spiritual foxes, wolves and lions - are mentioned many times in Scripture, and a quick look at nature assures us that it is far safer to mingle with the flock than to set out on our own. I can think of several examples of times when I was attacked by the enemy; all of them were situations in which I was alone or didn't talk to a trusted friend first.

Even the greatest Old Testament prophets like Elijah and Samuel didn't act on their own. They participated in training schools or mentoring which helped them hone their skills in the area of hearing God. Christ also demonstrated discipleship of his followers, spending most of His waking hours with those He trained. It is "by reason of use" (Hebrews 5:13-14) that our senses are trained to discern both good and evil.

We are called to fellowship and mutual accountability with others. This is not just for our safety, but for our maturity:

And He Himself gave some to be apostles, some prophets, some evangelists, and some pastors and teachers, for the equipping of the saints for the work of ministry, for the edifying of the body of Christ, till we all come to the unity of the faith and of the knowledge of the Son of God...that we should no longer be

children, tossed to and fro and carried about by every wind of doctrine, by the trickery of men, in the cunning craftiness of deceitful plotting, but speaking the truth in love, may grow up in all things into Him who is the head - Christ.
Ephesians 4:11-15, NKJV

We grow in fellowship with others, and we need the witness and counsel of those around us to help us discern whether what we hear is "right on."

3. Look for Confirmations

That said, there *are* times when God will ask us to do something that is atypical, that goes against the crowd. In these cases, we are justified in asking God for confirmation. *Just as it is the work of the Holy Spirit to draw us to Christ, it is the work of God to confirm the Word of Christ in us, with signs and wonders if needed.* I regularly ask God to confirm things for me, and there are plenty of Scriptural precedents for this. He is a loving God who backs up what we do in faith and does not let us wander too far off track. We do not need to fear that we will "miss it!" He is so much bigger, and He knows our hearts.

As you begin your journey of prayer, pray that the Lord will reveal any areas where religious tradition or personal fear has kept you from hearing His wonderful voice. If you have given up on hearing God because someone in authority told you it wasn't possible or you "heard wrong," I pray you will have the grace to forgive – and then return to the place where you left off in God. Familiarize yourself again with the sweet whispers of His voice. Let the Holy Spirit write His "Inscriptions" on the tablet of your heart.

2

KITCHEN SINK PRAYERS

"And pray in the Spirit with all kinds of prayers and requests. With this in mind, be alert and always keep on praying for all the Lord's people." ~Ephesians 6:18, NIV

I have always loved to pray. From the time I was a small child I believed that there was a God who could hear me. I talked to Him, read Bible stories about Him, and eventually gave my life to Him. For someone living with partial deafness, it was nice to know that God was one of the few people I could always hear.

Like all introverts, I prefer deeper relationships with a few people rather than surface relationships with many. So my praying also tended to be "deep," in the sense that I focused best on God when I had extended times of uninterrupted quiet and stillness. I didn't know that there were "varieties" of prayers that could be offered, or other "kinds" of prayers as Ephesians 6 describes above.

For a while, even as a single young adult, this was not a problem. Of course, I worked during the day and had other commitments to attend to, but I cultivated a deep relationship with God in my "off" hours. Sundays especially were devoted to Him: church was followed by hours of blissful peace in my quiet apartment, doing what I now laughingly call "swooning with Jesus!"

Then I fell in love and got married.

Suddenly, I was swooning over my husband, not Jesus, and had much less time to pursue my heavenly Bridegroom. Gradually, new demands encroached on my old prayer times: urgent things like laundry, dishes, and crying babies. Shopping trips took two hours now instead of twenty minutes, and I was falling in bed exhausted at night, wondering where the time had gone and how I would ever connect "deeply" with God again! God became just another task on my long "to-do" list, someone to whom I really couldn't give enough quality time. As any stay-at-home mom will tell you, there is just as much work at home as there is in the office; the only difference is that toddlers are tougher bosses!

The Spiritual Giant

It was around this time that I was leaving my church one Sunday morning, heading down to the nursery to pick up my children. Suddenly, my path was blocked by one of the church intercessors. Tall, slender, and with a sparkling smile, she stared down at me. I knew from what others said about her that her spiritual stature was as lofty as her physical height. One look at this "faith giant" reduced me. Next to her, I felt small, decidedly *UN*-sparkly, and spiritually insignificant!

I didn't realize until years later that our meeting was a divine appointment. God stood this seasoned warrior in my path that day as surely as the Angel of the Lord stood in front of Balaam's donkey to block his way. Her message changed my entire perspective on prayer.

The Power of a Kitchen Sink Prayer

When I bemoaned my lack of time to pray with this intercessor, she was nothing short of amazed. "Whatever made you think that you would have that kind of extended time with the Lord in this season of your life?" she asked. As she continued, I realized that

God had brought me into a new season, a new assignment in my spiritual life, but I was still trying to use methods from the old season that didn't work anymore. I was burdening myself with expectations I couldn't meet, expectations which were no longer part of the Holy Spirit's plan for me at the time.

"What you need to realize is that your prayers at the kitchen sink are every bit as effective as your prayers in the prayer closet," she added. "You may not have those four-hour stretches to intercede any longer, but you will learn to pray shorter, more effective prayers as you go through your days with children." Thanks to her, I did.

Discerning the Times

"Even the stork in the sky knows her appointed seasons, and the dove, the swift and the thrush observe the time of their migration. But My people do not know..." (Jer. 8:7, NIV) In the New Testament, Jesus laments that religious leaders cannot discern the signs of the times. (Matthew 16:3.)

Christians often have set ideas of what spirituality should look like. For me, it was the idea that a *good* prayer time had to be a *long* prayer time. For someone else, it might be the idea that relentless service is the measure of maturity. Regardless, holding on to old "wineskins," or previous ways of doing things, won't work when God changes our assignment or moves us into a new season. While long prayer times and faithful service are both *good* things, they will hinder us if the Holy Spirit is moving us on to something new and different. Remember, the measure of our spirituality is not in the type of service we offer, but in our love for Him and for those around us.

New seasons and changes of assignments keep us humble and flexible spiritually. They allow us to stretch our faith as we lean on God for new things. They sharpen our skills as we learn to love in new ways. The trick is in recognizing and adjusting to the new things He is doing! For this reason alone, we need to pray "all kinds of prayers."

I learned to sharpen my prayers as I washed my knives. The kitchen sink reminded me to wash my family with the water of the Word, and I still pray over each one today as I wash their dishes or clothes. I pray they will taste and see the goodness of the Lord. (Psalm 34:8.) I pray they will be clothed with power from on high (Luke 24:49) and with robes of righteousness (Isaiah 61:10). The kitchen sink, where I spent so much time, became my sanctuary.

Several years later, when I was well into this new family routine, my husband took a night job to help make ends meet. He worked from 3-11 pm, and my young children went to bed around 7 pm. Once again, my prayer assignment changed. I now had several hours of "quiet time" each night, and the Lord specifically instructed me to set aside that time for Him in prayer. He opened up a way for me to rediscover that precious extended time in His Presence. Not long after that, He gave me a promotion, this time to a prayer team I had longed to join but could not before. I rejoiced in the extended times of prayer, but I was also aware that the short "kitchen sink prayers" had honed me as an intercessor, making me much more effective.

In every season, God can make a way for you to grow as a prayer warrior, until you, too, become a "giant" in the faith. The answers to our quick, shorter prayers in the midst of the business of loving people are every bit as powerful and exciting as the answers to the ones we have labored over. I have found that I am not alone in praying "kitchen sink prayers," although others might call them by a different name. Here are just a few:

* Kitchen Sink Prayers: Use daily chore times to pray over family members or prayer requests. Wash your family with the water of the Word! (Ephesians.6:18; 5:26)

* Traffic Light Prayers: Pray for someone or some specific issue each time you stop at a red light. (See Matthew 20:32)

* Phone Prayers: Call a friend each morning and pray together for 15 minutes before starting your day. (Hebrews 10:24-25)

* Travel Prayers: Those who are on the road for business often can keep a list of prayer requests to pray about as they drive or commute. I know someone who kept a copy of the church directory in his car for years, and prayed for each church member by name as he drove daily to his sales calls. (Luke 24:13-17)

* Lunch Break Prayers: Use your lunch break to pray and fast occasionally. (Isaiah 58:4-5)

* Couple Prayers: Set aside a night or two each week to pray with your spouse. (1 Peter 3:7)

* Worshipful Prayers: Turn on worship music and dance, sing and pray - great with small children! (Ephesians 5:19)

* Family Prayers: When children are too young to leave you alone, include them in your quiet times. Purchase a children's Bible or coloring pages and teach them how to have their own quiet time with you. (Deuteronomy 11:19)

* Shower Prayers: Don't laugh! A friend of mine shared once that this is the best place she connects with God! (2 Corinthians 7:1)

* Parked Car Prayers: In a pinch, when you need to be alone, you can escape to your car, even if it is just parked in the driveway. No one will hear you, and you're still close enough to respond to emergencies. (Matthew 6:5-6)

* **Prayer Walks:** By far one of my favorite ways to pray, since exercising the body helps stimulate the mind as well. Pray for neighbors, family, church, or whatever the Lord leads as you walk. (Acts 3:1-8)

***Waiting Room Prayers:** Much of life is spent waiting. I have written entire articles in the dentist's office, waiting for my children, but the time could be spent praying or reading the Bible on your phone just as easily. Be creative! (Psalm 37:7)

* **"Trigger Prayers:"** Every time I see an ambulance, I pray for whoever is inside. Seeing the ambulance is a "trigger," a reminder for me to cover those who are in medical distress. You can use anything that inspires you to pray: an office building to remind you to pray for Christian businessmen, a school to remind you to pray for the safety, growth, and protection of your children. Be creative! (James 5:16)

* **Middle-of-the-Night Prayers:** Can't sleep? Do some damage to the enemy! These quiet hours are often the best time to connect peacefully with the Lord. (See Acts 16:25-27.) Pray through whatever comes to mind. (Philippians 4:6-7.) I use the nighttime hours to pray for pastors, the persecuted church, and those who might be suffering with illnesses or anxieties that keep *them* up at night. (Hebrews 13:3)

* **Constant Prayers:** (1 Thessalonians 5:17) As a Spirit-filled believer, you have an advantage: you can pray anytime, anywhere in the Spirit (i.e., in tongues), even quietly, to create a sacred place.

Apply This!

1. Think for a moment about the time and season you are in. Is God moving you into something new? Do things feel "out of sync" spiritually? How can you reorganize your prayer times OR the types of prayer you use to meet the demands of your new schedule or season? Be specific.

2. From the list above, which type of prayer most appeals to you? What have you tried that has been successful? If possible, choose one new way of praying and give it a try.

3
HOW TO DEVELOP A LIFESTYLE OF PRAYER: AN INTERVIEW WITH PASTOR JASON MCGEE

Jason McGee is the Senior Pastor of One Family Church in Shrewsbury, MA. My husband and I have known Jason and his family for years, and helped him plant his church in Shrewsbury.

One of the things that most impressed me during the church plant was his emphasis on prayer. I was curious to know, several years later, how he views prayer and what priority he gives to prayer in his growing congregation. Here are his thoughts.

"One of the few recorded requests the disciples made of Jesus was that He teach them how to pray," Pastor Jason notes. "This is how we know the Lord's Prayer. But most of the praying Jesus did in Scripture was done in private. Jesus rarely prayed in public.

Instead, He ministered to people out of the wisdom He received from the Father in private."

Jason's comments made me think more deeply about Christ's quiet times. We know little about Christ's prayer life, except that He often withdrew to listen to His Father and commune with Him. He received His instructions during those times. But prayer **was** mostly private and alone. The longest recorded conversations we have between Jesus and His Father are found in John, just prior to His death. There He revealed much more about how He prayed for His followers and Himself. (See Jesus's prayer in John 17.)

No Prayer, No Ministry.

I asked Pastor Jason whether he had focused on prayer in his time at seminary.

"In all my time at Bible School I don't remember *ever* taking a class on prayer, or hearing a teaching on prayer," Pastor Jason remarks. "I didn't really learn the value of prayer until more recently, maybe in the last 10 years or so. I met a lawyer from Puerto Rico who intrigued me; I saw something in him that I had not seen before, and I asked to sit with him. In listening to him, I learned to listen to God, to go slower. It transformed my prayer life.

"Later, another teacher invited me to his church, where I heard him pray out loud. I learned from him, and the Holy Spirit began teaching me about prayer on my own."

Pastor Jason says that now, prayer and the study of the Word are one and the same. Prayer and worship are also inseparable; for him, it is all about wholeheartedness and unity.

"When we want to commune with Jesus," Pastor Jason says, "we can go to the Word and pray through the scriptures – because HE IS the Word! We interact with Him over His Words and we worship Him with our responses – our prayers. I listen more than I speak. And the primary way God speaks is through His Word."

To emphasize the value of the Word, Jason reminds me of the story of the woman at the well. "Jesus said to her, 'If you knew the gift of God, and who it is who says to you, 'Give Me a drink,' you would have asked Him, and He would have given you living water.'" (John 4:10, NASB)

"We must realize that Jesus IS the Word, and we have communion with Him. That Samaritan woman *became the well* to her community, drawing others to Christ, because she communed with Him first. Without prayer, without communion, there will be no true ministry. It will just be you working in your own strength. Power comes through *listening* prayer. And neither prayer nor ministry happens without the Word."

To highlight the importance of listening, Pastor Jason cites the story of Peter, James and John on the mountaintop with Jesus, who was there to pray. (See Luke 9:28-36.) During this encounter, Peter quickly jumps in and speaks, wanting to build tabernacles for Jesus, Moses and Elijah. While he is speaking, a cloud overshadows him, and a voice says, "This is My Son, My Chosen One! *Listen* to Him!" (NLT) In our zeal to speak, we often neglect to listen.

Corporate Prayer Inspires Private Prayer

Pastor Jason recognizes that even in his own church, most people do not pray on their own. This is one reason why he begins every service with corporate prayer.

Jason believes that praying together during the service provides two benefits: first, it gives people a model for praying as they learn from listening to the prayers of others; people learn by example. Second, it creates unity. "Unifying lives in Christ is the mission of the church," Jason says. We are to put on love daily, to have communion and fellowship with God and each other, which brings unity."

Jason invites people to gather for a once-monthly prayer meeting, which his core leaders usually attend, and he also prays weekly with his elders. Typically, these are smaller meetings.

"Do you wish attendance at prayer meetings were greater?" I ask.

"Absolutely!" he says. "But even Jesus only took three of his disciples to the top of the mountain, and these same three fell asleep at Gethsemane! We don't see any of Christ's disciples praying actively on their own until after the resurrection, when Peter is seeing visions on rooftops, James is writing about how to pray for healing, and John is getting revelations on Patmos."

Prayer Releases Creativity

I asked Pastor Jason what seemed, at this point, to be a redundant question. Jason is an anointed preacher of God's Word, and when he speaks there is a depth and authority to his teaching that is rare even in Christian communities. My hunch was that his powerful preaching was directly related to a powerful prayer life. Was it true?

"I need to hear from the Lord," Jason replied. "It's not about what I have to say! There must be less of me speaking and more of Him. Power in ministry comes from alone time; the corporate is always a reflection of the private. We must pray on our own in order to make an impact corporately.

"God is a creative God," he states. "His Words are creative. When I get those words in me, I become creative, too!"

Typically, Pastor Jason spends time meditating on the Word throughout the week to prepare for his sermons. He finds that his preparation time for ministry boils down to two essential methods: a slow, word-by-word study of Bible passages which often lead him into other related scriptures; and what he calls "encounter" passages, where he puts himself in the position of someone in the Bible story in order to understand it better. "I ask myself, 'How would this person feel? What were they thinking?' I try to *become* the character in my mind, which opens up new revelation for me about the passage."

Prayer is Easier Than You Think

"What do you wish people knew about prayer?" I asked Pastor Jason as we finished our interview.

"That it's *easy*," he replied. "When you're aware of God, or thinking of Him, you're praying, because He's right there. We don't need to follow a protocol, like in the Old Testament, to enter into His Presence, because He is always with us! Psalm 46:10 says, 'Be still and know that I am God.' Prayer is more listening than talking; it is being aware of His nearness to us.

I am always inspired listening to others describe their quiet times with the Lord. For Pastor Jason, "quiet time" doesn't stop after his morning devotions. He is constantly *listening* for God, and it shows.

Apply This!

~ Who do you know who has a strong prayer life? Have you considered asking to pray with them, as Jason did, or talking about prayer over a cup of coffee? This is a powerful way to broaden your prayer life.

~ How much of your prayer time is spent listening? Talking? Do you pray with your Bible open or closed? Are you interacting with Jesus, the Word? Consider keeping your Bible open during prayer times and asking the Holy Spirit to reveal His Word to you as you read and pray!

~ Does your church currently pray together? Do you attend the prayer meetings your leaders initiate? Why or why not? How can you make prayer a higher priority in your daily life – or your church's life?

4

THE POWER OF SPIRITUAL DISCIPLINE

I have a confession to make. There are days when I just don't *want* to pray. Or write. Or do anything "spiritual." I'm not alone. Pastors have days when they just don't want to deal with another person, or another problem. Moms and dads just can't fathom dragging their kids through another tedious family devotion.

Don't get me wrong. I love prayer. I love all things related to the Lord and His Spirit. I love celebrating what He has done for us and getting to know Him, and His people, better. But I am just tired sometimes. My flesh cries out for "downtime," for a place where I am relieved of responsibility and free to just "be."

I had such a day this week. Family life was draining me: there was a difficult doctor's appointment for one child, a busy college application season for my senior, a hectic schedule for my husband. Mounds of laundry were piled up on not just one couch but two, waiting for someone to fold it. I had avoided the gym. Dinner was not made. I had managed, thankfully, to squeeze in a decent quiet time, but I had writing to do and was decidedly *un*inspired. *Un*spiritual. *Un*motivated! I just couldn't seem to find the energy to press on, spiritually. Going grocery shopping seemed more enticing than listening to the Lord!

But I didn't.

In a last-ditch effort to pull myself up by my own bootstraps, I sat down – *"just for a minute,"* I told myself – to be with the Lord. I confess I was desperate to hear something – *anything* – that would help me locate my spiritual "get up and go" again. Where had it gone? I wasn't going from glory to glory anymore, and I knew it. I just wanted a *break!*

Then God spoke.

A quick image, a thought flickered through my mind. I saw my spiritual life as if it were the life of an athlete. This brought everything back into perspective.

Spiritually, we are like reluctant athletes sometimes. We know we need to go back to the gym and maintain the discipline of steady workouts. We know we'll become stronger with regular exercise, increasing weights, and a healthy lifestyle. It takes work and commitment. *But our flesh doesn't want to!*

Like beginners, we "would-be athletes" crave rest in between our workouts at the gym. Maybe too much so. We're sore. Tired. That is to be expected. But just as too much time away from the gym causes our physical muscles to atrophy, so too much time away from the Lord weakens us spiritually.

Our dedication to the training process is as important spiritually as it is physically. A true athlete doesn't avoid the gym just because he feels tired or his muscles are a little sore from the last workout. He recognizes that these are symptoms of *growth*, not decay. Muscles are being built in his body. Dedication and perseverance are being formed in his mind.

When we make a commitment to be disciplined in the Spirit, we progress to maturity much faster. The trouble for us, as the apostle Paul said, is that we know what to do, but we don't do it!

As I listened to the Lord, He said, "Set aside time to pray and write, and I will meet you there." When we are tired and weary, we can rejoice in the fact that HE is faithful. We have a covenant relationship with a wonderful, powerful God. When we simply position ourselves to be with God, in whatever capacity He has called us to: counseling, writing, praying, or parenting, He meets us there. God upholds His end of the covenant and pours out grace and mercy when we need it most. It is a *good deal!*

If you're feeling spiritually drained or unmotivated today, I encourage you not to give up! Don't believe the enemy's lie that you are missing it, failing, or beyond hope. All you need to do is get yourself back to the "gym." Stop what you're doing, pick up your Bible, and position yourself so that you can just listen to the Lord for a moment. You might have forgotten Him, but He has not forgotten you! (Isaiah 49:16.) He will meet you there.

There is power in spiritual discipline. Because I positioned myself before Him, a simple thought from the Lord changed my entire outlook on an otherwise dreary day. The more I do this, the more I hear Him. I'm praying that a simple reminder to be disciplined in your commitment to your quiet times with the Lord will give you the jump-start you need, too. May you go from glory to glory and strength to strength!

5
JESUS IS THE HIGHWAY, NOT THE DETOUR!

For thus said the Lord GOD, the Holy One of Israel, "In returning and rest you shall be saved; in quietness and in trust shall be your strength." But you were unwilling.
~Isaiah 30:15, ESV

If you're anything like me, you tend to become sidetracked from prayer, on a regular basis, by the "stuff" of life. Work, family, friends in need, and even church obligations pull at us constantly, demanding our immediate attention. It isn't always easy to pray.

The real power to live life victoriously is found in our *consistency*. Consistent efforts in any area – professional, religious or otherwise – yield success. We cannot expect to reap a harvest where we have not sown! In fact, it is this law – the law of sowing and reaping –

that the Lord says will endure *forever*. (Genesis 8:22.) Like the law of gravity, its application is timeless, its results guaranteed.

Why, then, do we so easily fail to be disciplined in our prayer lives, when we know that consistency will produce a great harvest for us?

Our reluctance is rooted in a wrong belief: that Jesus is a detour, not the highway.

"I Just Don't Have Time to Pray!"

Think about it. You wake up on Monday morning. You spent yesterday at church, so you are feeling renewed, refreshed, and ready to tackle the week ahead. The pastor's inspiring sermon is still ringing in your head, and you have plans – *big plans* – to make an impact for Jesus in your home or workplace.
"Change *is* possible," you think, "I just need to *do* what I've heard preached all these years."

Full of ideas and plans for the week ahead, you decide you don't really *need* to take the time to sit and pray today. God is with you,

you think, and you need to make use of as much of your free time as you can before you get to work. Sitting down for an hour to pray would derail you, slow you down. You don't have time for "detours" right now.

So you launch into your list of tasks and get a head start on the day's events. You plow energetically through Monday, and then Tuesday, and by "hump day" you realize something is off. YOU are off. Off track, that is! In your excitement to "get things done," you neglected to really listen for the Lord or focus on His Word. Sure, you played some worship music in your car on the way to and from work, but now you're feeling drained, tired, maybe even overwhelmed because your list is still as long as it was on Monday, but your energy is coming up short.

"I Think God is Mad At Me..."

At this point, the enemy sees an opportunity. He quietly suggests to you that you have *really* missed it. "*Three days* without God!" He chastens. "Tsk, tsk! God must be mad at you." Suddenly, you feel guilty. You're not much of a Christian, are you? Why can't you just maintain a regular quiet time, like everybody else?!

The truth is, everybody else struggles with this, too, because we all share a common enemy. We all live in the same busy world. And invariably, we all reach the same conclusion: *being with Jesus feels more like a "detour" in our life than a highway.*

How Do I Change Direction?

I have felt the same way. As I've shared in previous posts, I am a strong "Type A" personality. I LOVE to-do lists, because I love the feeling of accomplishment I get when I finish them! To put it simply, I am already consistent and disciplined in my life – *but not always in the right areas.*

To change direction, I have had to renew my thinking to see things God's way. *People*, not tasks, are the priority. *Love* is the standard of measurement for believers: not whether we finished our lists, evangelized the masses, or raised successful children. It is **relationships** that are key: with Jesus, first, then with the people around us. Thankfully, I've learned to apply the same discipline I have in my "workaholic" personality to maintaining a consistent time of prayer.

It has not been easy. Relationships, with all their messiness, can feel like detours.

Jesus confronted me about this one day. He said, **"I am the highway, not the detour!"** I saw, in that instant, that I placed a lower value on knowing God than I should. The apostle Paul said his *greatest desire* was to "know Him [Jesus], and the power of His resurrection…" (Philippians 3:10) Sadly, I could not say at that time that this was true for me.

Many of us feel pressured to hurry through life. We are programmed to avoid detours, or what we perceive as such. Our GPS warns us when something on our route will slow us down. Caller ID notifies us in advance of calls we'd rather avoid. Often life's "detours" look a lot like people: *relationships.* We feel that anything that stands in our way prevents us from reaching our destiny. Or does it?

When Paul was kept under house arrest for two years, was it a detour, or destiny? God used people who opposed Paul to multiply His Word in Rome. In fact, Paul's boldness while imprisoned empowered many other believers to preach boldly, too.

When Jesus was crucified, was He being **prevented** from doing His ministry or **propelled** into the most magnificent ministry of all: the resurrection?

When the believers in the early church (Acts 4) took the time to pray after being threatened by the authorities, were they taking time **away** from ministry or **contributing** to it?

The Bible tells us that after these believers prayed, revival broke out. The building was shaken, *everyone* was filled with the Holy Spirit, and with "great power" and renewed boldness believers testified about the resurrection of Jesus!

Take the Highway!

The time we take to develop our relationship with Jesus is not a detour. It's a highway. Sowing to the Spirit reaps rewards we cannot manufacture in our own strength. Our minds are renewed. Our energy is restored. Our time is multiplied. And our tasks become easier. After all, look at the community in Acts 4. Is it easier to pray for people one by one to receive the Holy Spirit, or for God to show up and fill everyone at once?! My vote is for the latter!

As you change your mindset to see your relationship with God and His people as a priority, you will see Him change your circumstances so that what needs to happen, happens more effectively. For a "Type A" person like me, there is nothing as exciting as that! I love that when I take care of God's business, He takes care of mine! We are partners, and partners talk. Partners plan together. Partners listen to each other, share ideas, and shape and refine their plans into something much greater than what one could do alone.

Make a fresh decision today to spend consistent quality time with your Lord. Put prayer on your calendar first! Nothing else compares. In fact, as Jesus told Martha, nothing else really matters! Over time, your diligent sowing will yield a harvest. Your thoughts will become enemy-proof. Your efforts will be more effective. Because when you pray, symbolically giving Jesus your meager loaves of bread, He blesses them, and multiplies them in ways that no mere man can reproduce.

6
DELIVERED, NOT DISAPPOINTED

Our fathers trusted in You; they trusted, and You delivered them.
They cried to You, and were delivered; they trusted in You, and
were not ashamed.
~Psalm 22:4-5, NKJV

There I was: eyes closed, hands raised, completely absorbed in the worship and the amazing spiritual atmosphere of the church. A powerful move of God had hit this place, and I was determined to press in and get my healing. Full of faith, I prayed in the Spirit. Others also prayed for me. The Presence of God was ***so strong*** in that meeting. It was unlike anything I had ever seen. And then...

Nothing happened.

I mean it. ***Nothing*** happened.

I remember sitting on the floor after the meeting ended, sobbing into someone's arms. I was *so disappointed*. God was there! How could He not heal me? I had _faith_! I had prayed! And even if I had no faith, others were praying for me. What happened?

It was a hard lesson to learn, and it took me several years to recover. *Years.* Because I thought God healed. (He does.) And I had hoped He would heal me. (But He didn't.) Not that night.

Dealing with Disappointment

If you're human, you probably have a story similar to mine. Or know someone who does. The death of a loved one, the loss of a job, or a healing *not* received can do serious damage to our faith. Many Christians turn their backs on God after such events, and it's easy to understand why.

It's disappointing when God doesn't come through for us like we hope He will. Life rarely turns out as we expect, but it's especially difficult when what we're hoping for is something God *says He will do* in the Bible. What then?

Unmet Expectations Lead to Disappointment

At the time of that meeting, if you had asked me, I would have told you that I was in a place of complete faith and trust in God. I had every confidence that God would come through for me; after all, healing is a part of the atonement. (See 1 Peter 2:24.) It wasn't until years later that I realized *my trust was not in God, but in my idea of what **I** thought God should do that night.* Apparently, He and I had different ideas about what was going to happen!

Any counselor will tell you that anger and disappointment are rooted in unmet expectations. When I compared *my* expectations to God's for that night, I came up short. It was God's will to heal me, but not at that time, nor in that way. In fact, He was healing something else I didn't even know was broken: my misplaced trust.

A Decision to Trust

Take Naaman, for example. This commander of the Syrian army heard that there was a prophet in Israel who could heal his leprosy. (2 Kings 5:1-14.) He took a servant's advice and traveled, with the king's permission, directly to the door of the prophet Elisha, in

Israel.

To his surprise, Elisha did not even come to the door, sending a messenger to him instead. "Go and wash in the Jordan seven times, and your flesh shall be restored to you, and you shall be clean." (2 Kings 5:10, NKJV.)

Sounds easy, right? Just take a few baths and you're healed! But Naaman became furious. Look at his reaction: "Indeed, I said to myself, 'He will surely come and stand and call on the name of the Lord his God, and wave his hand over the place, and heal the leprosy.'" (2 Kings 5:11.) In fact, Naaman was extremely angry that Elisha would expect him to wash in an *Israelite* river, instead of the "superior" waters of Syria!

Naaman's elaborate idea of what God should do got in the way of his healing. Unmet expectations gave way to anger and pride, and had his servants not intervened, Naaman's story would have ended without a healing, too. Thankfully, he repented and did as Elisha asked. When he followed God's plan, he was healed immediately. The key was his decision to trust God's plan instead of his own.

Delivered from Disappointment

Romans 5:5 tells us that God-centered hope does not disappoint us because of His love for us. That's a pretty powerful statement from Father God to His children! God *is* love, and His plan for us is one that includes deliverance from disappointment. How, then, do we reconcile what we read in His Word with our life experiences?

Like Naaman, we need to shift our expectations. When anger and disappointment rise up on the inside, we need to take a better look on the outside to see what God is really up to. Disappointment is a signal to us that something is not right, that our trust is in something other than God.

If you are a Christian, you are appointed to celebrations of deliverance, to the joy of answered prayer, and to godly, fulfilled dreams! (See John 15:16, Leviticus 23, and Habakkuk 2:3.) When God commanded Israel to celebrate annual feasts, He EXPECTED that they would have something to celebrate! Whether it was their deliverance from slavery, the annual harvest, the Sabbaths, or a Jubilee year, the fact that these feasts were to be celebrated *perpetually* tells us that God has **good** plans for us ALL the time!

Detours to Deliverance

In the early 1990's, I went through an extended period of intense healing and deliverance. For roughly two years, God worked a major overhaul in my life, rooting out sin, dealing with wrong beliefs, walking me through forgiveness, and yes, healing a *lot* of disappointment.

During that time, my spiritual mother and father would often surprise me by "kidnapping" me. (Which wasn't as bad as it sounds, I promise!) To break the intensity of our work, they would pack their car with snacks and drinks, put my weary body in the back seat, and drive to an "undisclosed" location. Sometimes it would be a castle or a state park; other days we'd visit the ocean; longer trips might take us North to lunch at a country store.

I never knew where we were going until we got there, and my constant guessing only added to the fun! These were all-day trips, and the travel time in the car became trust-building time. Often mom would fall asleep on the way home, and I remember having long, deep spiritual conversations with my father that could really not have happened any other place. I grew to love these times, because I trusted my spiritual dad implicitly and knew that I'd come back refreshed from our "adventures."

If we encountered a detour, forgot the food, or had problems along the way, my parents would always say, "That doesn't matter. What matters is that we're together."

As I've grown, I've come to realize that when life deals us detours or disappointments, our heavenly Father is often wanting to give deliverance to His kids, too. He's longing for us to get out of the driver's seat, move to the back, and let Him navigate. He's looking for the deeper conversations where we share our bitter disappointments, our harder questions, and even our angry weariness with Him. It is in this way that our trust in Him is built and deliverance is secured.

God has both the destination *and* the plans for your life in His hand. Because He loves, you, He doesn't want to disappoint you; His goal is to surprise you with a deliverance you could never dream of yourself! When Israel left Egypt, they didn't just run for their lives; they ran off with all the Egyptians' silver and gold, too! When we let *God* write the story, He gets the glory!

If you are struggling with disappointment today, please pray this prayer with me, expecting your deliverance!

God, I come to you weary, disappointed, and very lost. I thought I

knew what You were doing and where we were going, but I really didn't. Please take the wheel of my life and get me back on course: YOUR course! I believe that no matter how far off the map I've gone, You know the way home, and it doesn't matter anyway. What matters is that we're together. Forgive me for taking control and crashing into disappointment! Help me to rest as You bring me to a better place. I choose to trust You, and I ask You to help me sort out all my questions along the way. I believe You have a great deliverance for me, one that will bring You honor and me joy. I believe Your blessing makes me rich, and there is no sorrow added to it. I trust You with my life. Amen.

"For I know the plans I have for you," declares the Lord, "plans to prosper you and not to harm you, plans to give you hope and a future."
~Jeremiah 29:11, NIV

Now hope does not disappoint, because the love of God has been poured out in our hearts by the Holy Spirit who was given to us.
~Romans 5:5, NKJV

7
HEAVEN'S COURTROOM

Imagine that you have just been issued a summons. You must appear in court immediately, and not as a juror. You have been called by the prosecution to take the stand as a defendant in a case with a high dollar value. If you lose, your sentence could include a lifetime in prison. What's worse: *you have been falsely accused.*

If it sounds like I am being dramatic, rest assured, I am not. The first paragraph is *entirely true.* As a Christian, you are – this very moment – being called by the devil (the prosecution) to take a defensive stand against his false accusations. He is, unfortunately, a very good lawyer, having practiced his craft since time began. Nevertheless, you have an excellent lawyer as well: your advocate, Jesus.

Now, I know you're on the right side of the law, and you know you're on the right side, but the prosecution wants to prove otherwise. If he succeeds, he gains access to your money, your mental and physical health, your family, or even your life. His goal is to lock you up for a lifetime.

Having a good lawyer will help, of course, but in this heavenly courtroom what matters most is your <u>testimony</u>. You are about to be tested on the facts, and whether your actions are legal. If you don't know your rights as a citizen of heaven, or if the enemy can find a weakness in your argument, you will lose the case.

As in any trial, you must have two weapons. The first is an excellent lawyer who is familiar with your case. If you're a Christian, you already have a good relationship with the best attorney there is in spiritual matters: Jesus Christ. In Him you are on the *right* side of the law, no matter what you have done. He has never lost a case. As long as you choose Him as your Advocate, you stand a pretty good chance of winning.

The second weapon is a detailed knowledge of the law, which in this case represents your covenant with God. This is where the prosecution often gains the upper hand, since you do not know the law as well as he does, nor are you used to defending yourself against such deceptive, unfair arguments. You will find that the prosecution has accessed information about your life that you did not wish to be made public. You will be horrified to hear that he can call to the witness stand, one by one, people who willingly testify against you, dragging past sins to the surface and making you look like a heartless criminal!

In the final analysis, it will be very important that what you do and say lines up with the law. Satan's legal strategy from the beginning has been to cast doubt on our words: "Did God really say…?" (Genesis 3:1-3.) Your best defense is going to be to stick to the words your attorney, Jesus, gives you to say, and avoid adding too much of your own.

"Isn't *that* deceptive," you might ask? After all, I really *am* guilty of a lot of things, and I don't always do what I should. What that witness said about me was true: I really *didn't* like the guy, and I treated him badly because I couldn't forgive him. I deserve punishment."

The question is, do you? You might have opened the door to some legal "loopholes" the prosecution is now using against you, but the real test is whether you believe *and can prove* that you are innocent. In a happier moment, it's easy to believe your mistakes are covered by the blood of Jesus, which ratifies your covenant with God. But when the opposition mounts, can you still stand on that testimony? Do you know which clauses in your contract validate what you have experienced spiritually?

Those who do cite them and win their cases. Those who don't have a harder time. Fortunately, Jesus knows what it's like to be a defendant on the courtroom stand. He was challenged twice: in the wilderness (Luke 4) and before His death (Luke 22-23:47). Both times He adhered to God's covenant and responded only with the Words of God. Both times, He won.

Jesus didn't allow his feelings to contaminate His testimony. Instead, He studied His covenant with God until He knew the law inside and out. He lived a legal, righteous life even when falsely accused. He accepted a death sentence from the enemy only because He knew that God would ultimately give him the keys to get out of that prison. He spoke only the words of the covenant and He fulfilled the law perfectly in His life on earth.

Believers are summoned daily to take the stand: not as those who have lived a perfect life, as Jesus did, but as those who are protected by *His* knowledge of and adherence to the law. Every time we are summoned, we should arrive at the courtroom with our

Bible contract in hand. Everything we say in our defense should be based on what Jesus, our attorney, outlines for us. We should stick to our testimony of His goodness like glue. Anything else we say can and will be used against us!

The more certain you are of your innocence in Christ and your rights as a believer, the more likely you are to live a blessed life.

If you feel you have been falsely accused by the enemy, pray this prayer today: **"Jesus, You are the most successful attorney I could ever have. I am so grateful that You know how to defend me against the trials and accusations the enemy uses against me. I have been falsely accused, Lord! Give me the time I need to sit down with you and review our covenant until I know it inside and out. Convince me of the blessings and freedom You have already won for me, so that my testimony holds up under every cross-examination. I praise You for your victories! I thank you that You have the keys to unlock every jail cell the enemy throws me into! We win!"**

"And if any man sin, we have an advocate with the Father, Jesus Christ the righteous. And He is the propitiation for our sins; and not for ours only, but also for the sins of the whole world.
1 John 2:1-2, KJV

8

HOW A "MINI" PRAYER RETREAT CAN RECONNECT YOU WITH GOD

No matter what your vision is, you will easily drift from that vision unless you take the time to develop an action plan that propels you towards your desired destination. "Drift" happens in your marriage, your vocation, or your spiritual life when you lose sight of your purpose and mission in those areas. Therefore, one of the best ways to stay focused spiritually is to develop an action plan.

Many people are frustrated that they don't seem to hear from God, and yet they never take specific steps to change that. Since we have a biblical promise that believers _can_ hear him (John 10:27), it's up to us to listen! If you are among those who aren't as disciplined about maintaining quiet times, or if you simply want to improve your existing relationship with God, this strategy is for you.

I challenge you to pull out your calendar, block off at least an hour or two of time in the near future (a half day would be even better), and do a "mini" prayer retreat. The goal of your retreat is to create an action plan that will help you see *exactly* how you can improve your relationship with God.

A sample "mini-retreat" outline (adapted from the book, <u>Living Forward</u> by Michael Hyatt & Daniel Harkavy) can be found at the end of this chapter. If you like, take a quick glance at it now, and I'll describe how it works for me personally as we progress.

Why Do a Prayer Retreat?

Because they are so powerful, I hold prayer retreats on a regular basis each year. Schedules and priorities change, and it is helpful to get away and "take inventory" to see where my spiritual resources are weak or depleted, and what areas need growth or change. Even disciplined believers with regular quiet times need a chance to evaluate occasionally what is working and whether they are moving closer to their ultimate goal of *Life-Giving Communication* with God in every area of life.

For example, one of the things I have noticed (and write about frequently on my blog) is my tendency to allow notifications on my phone to distract me from my focus. Looking at the retreat outline above, that habit falls under the category of my "present reality."

However, the kind of future I envision with God is similar to the one I cultivate with friends: *if I am having a conversation with someone, I put the phone away and focus on the relationship.* I'd like to be more consistent in really listening to God, and this can't happen when I'm pulled away by phone calls or emails every few minutes.

So to reach the goal of giving God my full attention, my specific action plan includes waiting until my quiet time is over before turning on my phone, and – to increase my focus during the day – returning to just a few set times daily when I check email and messages. *I have learned that very few alerts on my phone demand my immediate attention, no matter how loud or persistent they seem!*

A second priority for me is increasing the amount of prayer time I spend listening to God. It is easy, and sometimes tempting, to read the Word, send up a few personal requests for the day, and then move on. My richest quiet times, however, come when I allow God the time to speak in return, quietly journaling what I hear Him saying to me, or even taking the time to meditate more deeply on the scripture verses He "highlights" to me as I read.

Tithe Your Time

If the idea of doing a mini prayer retreat interests you, make a commitment to God *right now* to schedule that time – *before you close this book and move on to the next things in your day!* It is much easier to move forward spiritually when you set aside just a little time at the outset to create a plan and stay focused.

My mission, and the mission of His Inscriptions, is to help you *"Discover Life-Giving Communication with God."* If you decide to use the prayer retreat outline above, I'd love to hear how it works for you.

In fact, I'm going to make this as personally powerful as I can: if you have set a date and time for your retreat, I would be delighted to pray for you on that day, so that you can feel confident that God is speaking to you. There is power in unified prayer!

Send me an email via the contact form on my website: www.HisInscriptions.com. Tell me the date and time you plan to do your retreat, and I and my team will agree with you in prayer.

Where to Do A Mini Prayer Retreat

There are many places to do spiritual retreats all around the world.

L'Abri is one well-known resource for Christians, with retreat centers in Massachusetts, Minnesota, Canada, England, Australia, Switzerland, Korea, and even Brazil. Founded by Francis Schaeffer, L'Abri offers comfortable homes (The French word "L'Abri" means "shelter") where guests spend half of each day in self-directed stufy and the other half working in the community. Dinnertime conversations and lectures are always spiritually focused and very enlightening! I have enjoyed many pleasant hours in both the American and Swiss retreat houses.

For a large database of retreat centers in the Northeast, try the RetreatFinder website. (Please be aware, however, that not all centers on this site are Christian.) Many Catholic monasteries open simple rooms for believers to rent daily or weekly to do quieter "monastic" retreats or to simply be part of a God-centered community.

To connect online with others who pray, I highly recommend Pray Network's website (www.Pray.Network.org), which also lists nationwide prayer events. I also post links to such events on my Facebook page for His Inscriptions. (Go to www.Facebook.com/HisInscriptions.)

Finally, check with churches in your local area for prayer rooms that are open to anyone wishing to use them. It is a rare church that will turn away someone who wants to invest time in prayer! These settings are usually quiet and conducive to personal reflection.

Even the simplest walk outdoors can give you an opportunity to talk with Jesus. The two disciples on the road to Emmaus (Luke 24) had an encounter with their Savior that changed them forever.

Ask the Lord to give you both the time and the place for your appointment with Him. Prayer is the best investment you can make.

MINI PRAYER RETREAT OUTLINE

What to Bring:

Bible, Notebook, Pen, Water/Snack

Location:

Choose a peaceful place where you will not be interrupted.
Can be an office with a door, a prayer room, a retreat center,
or a scenic spot outdoors. Turn off / leave behind all electronics!

Dedicate Your Time:

Begin with prayer or praise. Give your time to the Lord, ask Him to
quiet your soul and open your ears to His voice.
Take authority over your mind, emotions, & every distraction
that hinders you from connecting with God.

Reflect on Your Spiritual Future:

What is your vision for your spiritual future with God?
What does it look like? Describe your desired or ideal relationship with
God in detail, using your imagination & senses. Write it down in the
present tense, documenting what you see. What are you doing in the
Kingdom? How do you communicate with Him?

Describe Your Present Reality

Take the next few minutes to write a detailed, honest assessment
of where you are in relationship to your envisioned future.
What works? What doesn't? What needs to change?

Create A Specific Action Plan

Make a list of specific, measurable, & realistic steps you can
take to move from your current reality to your envisioned future with
God. If you work 9-5, spending 3 hours a day in prayer or Bible study is
unlikely! A private lunch hour with God 3x/week is a better goal.
Include a time limit for reaching or practicing each goal.

Dig Into Scripture

Find one or more specific Bible verses that reinforce your vision and
motivate or inspire you. Examples: Colossians 1:9-11; John 10:27; 14:12;
1 John 5:14-15; Psalm 1; Psalm 119:15; Ephesians 3:14-21

Close with Prayer & Thanksgiving

9
ARE YOU LISTENING?

Once, the Lord gave me a prophetic word through a very personal analogy. He showed me that when the churches don't allow Him to speak, we develop a profound spiritual hearing loss, similar to what I have dealt with in the natural for most of my life. Let me explain by sharing what it means *not to hear,* and then give you a vision for what it would be to hear Him more clearly.

What Did You Say?

I have about a 70% hearing loss in both ears. It is a nerve loss that man cannot cure. (Although healing it is no problem for God!)

This means that for half a century (yes, I'm that young!), I have struggled on a daily basis to discern what people are saying to me, piecing together parts of conversations, reading lips and studying body postures if necessary, to add to my understanding. It is one of the reasons why I much prefer a book to a conversation, because then I know I will comprehend the whole thing, not just pieces of it!

I have always felt that the most precious gift I could give you is to listen to you, and to hear you. To this end, I have spent countless hours ministering to people in crisis, listening, counseling, and praying. And I *haven't* heard every word, but I *have* listened, and I have loved, and I have tried to show people that they are valued and *heard*, because God did the same for me. By God's grace, the land of my need has become the land of my anointing.

The problem, obviously, is that the struggle just to <u>hear</u> can be highly stressful.

When we married, my husband gave me the gift of being a stay-at-home mom. I used this time to develop greater intimacy with God. I had always loved prayer, but the freedom not to work gave me the time I needed to listen to God more regularly and get to know His voice.

His Sheep Hear His Voice

The beautiful thing about God's voice is that everyone can hear it!

(John 10:27.) *Even someone who is deaf can still "hear" the promptings of the Spirit.* Our ability to hear in the natural has no bearing on our ability to hear in the Spirit. In fact, God chastises His people through Jeremiah, Ezekiel, *and* Jesus for having ears but not hearing, and eyes but not seeing. (See Jeremiah 5:21, Ezekiel 12:2, and Matthew 13:13.)

When I spend time listening to the One whose voice I *can* hear, He releases me from the stress and anxieties that come from not being able to *rest*- the striving that comes from trying to hear voices that always seem too soft.

The Church's Hearing Loss

The analogy for the church is this: just as my stress level increases when I cannot hear people; in the same way, the church is stressed when the noise of our serving hinders the ease of our listening. While God is certainly capable of thundering from heaven, He tends to speak in quieter whispers. It is rare to find a church whose Sunday services allow time for God to speak; we are moving at an astonishing pace, and the noise is deafening. Our relentless programs and agendas prohibit us from developing the intimacy and relationship we need with our King. The devil knows that intimacy is the very place where healing and rest occur.

We need the healing that comes from hearing. The church becomes sick, tired, and broken down when we are so busy serving Him that we do not make it a priority – corporately or individually - to hear from Him. "Come to Me," He says in Matthew 11:28, "all you who labor and are heavy laden, and I will give you rest."

I am saddened by our tendency to drown out the voice of God with the noise of our own agendas. If our service means that we have no time to seek God and hear His instructions, then our ministries will soon fail. Our preoccupation with our to-do lists and agendas is in vain because it is ultimately only the wishes of the King that matter. This can be a hard concept for people in democratic nations to grasp. We don't understand the weight or the priority of a king's word.

Hearing and Healing

In over 30 years of ministry in various denominations, I have been the most blessed by people and churches who have shown true respect for the voice of our heavenly King. I'm not just talking about the difference between those who allow prophecy and those who do not. I'm noticing that there are those who have chosen to make listening to God a priority.

I think of one pastor I know who does not venture an opinion or do any ministry without first listening for God's instructions. I know of one church that worships its way into the Presence of God and then waits silently to let God speak before beginning their planned sermons and programs.

I know from talking with many stressed, unfocused Christians that they long to hear and do what God has created them to do, not just what man has asked them to participate in. They simply aren't sure how to do it or where to start.

I believe that our Sovereign King, the One who holds in His hands the blueprints for how to build the church, may be wondering what it is we think we are building without Him. He may be waiting for us to wait on Him, to embrace Him closely enough to hear His heartbeat. He may be speaking to us ever so softly, asking, "Are you listening?"

10
BE A SPIRITUAL LIFEGUARD

Leaders in the Body of Christ are called, among other things, to be lifeguards. *Watching* is the key function of a prophet or intercessor. *Rescuing* is a priority for the evangelist. *Guarding* is elementary for the pastor. *Warning* is a main component of teaching. *Vision* is essential for the apostle. Believers in the Kingdom of God are expected to be on guard, or more specifically: to keep watch.

My pastor runs a waterskiing ministry at the lake near his church in the summertime. On days when he is alone, the kids know that if he is out on the water training someone, *no one swims* until he gets back to the dock.

I visited one day, offering to watch the children who stayed behind to swim while he took a handful of others out on his boat. Some of the kids were eager but inexperienced swimmers. He asked me only one question before he left: *"Are you ready to dive in and save them if someone is in trouble?"*

I was.

I thought nothing of his question at the time, since I had grown up around the water and understood the risks involved. My pastor's question didn't stand out to me until I began writing this chapter. The pastor didn't realize it, but he had summed up the concept of <u>spiritual</u> lifeguarding in one sentence.

We need spiritual lifeguards: people who are ready to lead, rescue, warn and save. Without them, we are at the mercy of dangers we have not foreseen. With them, we are safe. We must learn to ***keep watch!***

What Are We Watching For?

Most of us know that we watch, foremost, for the return of our Lord Jesus Christ. While no one knows the day or hour, the Bible trains us to look for specific signs that alert us to His coming. (See Matthew 24.) Yet this is not the only thing we watch for!

Just like a lifeguard at the ocean, we are also watching *for immediate dangers, both internal and external.* It isn't just the enemy who threatens us, as in shark-infested waters, but fellow believers who get in "over their heads," so to speak.

Believers often overestimate their abilities to withstand temptation and may need warnings concerning the potential threats of sin. Like an inexperienced swimmer pulled under by the tides or waves, we need to notice the conditions of those around us, and be ready to save.

This isn't always easy. A spiritual drowning can be as sudden and silent as a natural one. Jesus says in Luke 21:34: "Be on guard..." (NASB.) Here are the types of things we are to watch for:

Spiritual Lifeguard's Watch List

Deception and erroneous doctrine (1 & 2 Timothy)

Dissipation, drunkenness, cares of life (Luke 21:34; Matt. 6; 2 Timothy 2:4)

Sin (Luke 17:3; John 5:16)

The enemy (Colossians 1:13; 1 Peter 5:8)

Temptation (2 Peter 2:9)

Yourself and the Church of God (Acts 20:28; Jude 1:23)

False Teachers (Ephesians 4:14; 1 Timothy 4:16)

Idols (1 John 5:21)

Straying from the Truth (2 Timothy 2:18)

Love of money (1 Timothy 6:9-11; 6:17)

Old Testament Lifeguards

Gatekeepers: God understood our need for protection, and the Old Testament is full of examples of spiritual lifeguards. We read of the gatekeepers in the tabernacle who were part of the Levitical priesthood, and served in shifts for seven days, guarding the temple and its wealth. (See 1 Chronicles 9). This was considered a "trusted office" (1 Chron. 9:26), an official position of responsibility requiring training and maturity.

There were also gatekeepers at all of Israel's camp entrances, and at the King's gate. Nehemiah noted that there were 284 Levites and 172 gatekeepers in his time. Earlier, there were even more listed: 1 Chronicles 23:5 records that four thousand men were designated as gatekeepers, with another four thousand as worshipers. This is no insignificant job in the Kingdom of God!

Watchmen: 2 Samuel 18 describes a second kind of lifeguard: the *watchmen*. One Hebrew word for "watch" is *shamar*, which means to hedge about as with thorns, guard; protect; beware; attend to; take heed; be circumspect; preserve; save. (*Strong's*

Concordance definitions.)

These watchmen have a threefold purpose: to STAND (on a high place or tower), to SEE (the messengers or enemies approaching), and to SAY (reporting to gatekeepers or kings what they saw as they watched). Their function is comparable to the prophetic office today. (Revelatory people work in conjunction with pastors and apostles, who give practical application to God's spiritual messages.) There are both human *and* angelic watchmen (see Daniel 4:13).

Ezekiel 33:1-12 is perhaps the clearest explanation of a watchman's responsibility: to *hear* God's words and *warn* His people. (See the full text for details.) Failure to do so resulted not just in deaths to the Israelites, but also to the prophet (or lifeguard) himself.

God puts it this way: "he who takes warning will save his life," but when someone dies for lack of a warning, "his blood I will require at the watchman's hand." He goes on to state further: "I have no pleasure in the death of the wicked… why should you die, O house of Israel?" (Ezekiel 33:5-6;11, NKJV.) God is in the business of saving lives, not losing them!

New Testament Lifeguards

Jesus is our best example of a New Testament lifeguard: He laid down His life for us so that we could pass from the kingdom of darkness to the Kingdom of God.

1 John 3:16 reads: *"By this we know love, because He (Jesus) laid down His life for us. And we also ought to lay down our lives for the brethren."* When Jesus Himself needed rescuing, God raised Him up and became His Son's "lifesaver" at the resurrection! (Hebrews 13:20.) *We're on a team of lifeguards who can walk on water and raise the dead!* Hallelujah!

The fivefold ministry functions of the church (found in Ephesians 4:11) also teach us how to operate as spiritual lifeguards. See where you fit in:

Apostles: these overseers watch the spiritual horizon for "big picture" opportunities and dangers in the Kingdom, things a local pastor might miss. **They have exchanged a local, microscopic view of one church for a regional or international perspective on the greater Body of Christ.** They're recruiting the next generation of leaders and training them for lifeguard duty. They're making sure that each new "lifeguard" understands the water, knows their own limitations, watches for common dangers, and blows the whistle when things get out of hand. They know when someone is ready to lay down his life for the perishing, and are well versed in every aspect of "lifesaving" known to the church. Scriptures include: Acts 20:28, 2 Corinthians 12:12; Luke 9:1.

Prophets: Our modern-day "watchmen," prophets (and often prayer warriors and intercessors) stand in the "high places" with God, listening and watching for incoming messages or approaching dangers to the church community. When they see, they speak. What they hear, they report. When God brings someone to their mind, they pray. **They know that *prayer and prophetic words are the life preservers* God has given them to toss out to those who are drowning.** Scripture includes: 1 John 5:16

Evangelists: Those gifted as evangelists take to heart the scripture in Jude 1:22-23: "Rescue others by snatching them from the flames of judgment..." (NLT). They understand that those not rescued from the fire today will spend eternity in the lake of fire (Rev.20:15). **The "life preserver" they use is a ready**

presentation of the Gospel, personal enough not to sound scripted and simple enough that a child could respond. They don't wait for someone to drown; they pray for divine appointments with those who can't swim, *before* they reach the water! Scriptures include: Jude 1:22-23; 2 Tim. 4:5; Colossians 1:13.

Pastors: Like shepherds, pastors are intimately attuned to the needs of their flocks. **Relationship is their floatation device**, extended to all who will respond. They watch for predators, such as those who would deceive church members. They are aware of the limitations of individual congregants, and can offer counsel when someone is in too deep or led astray. They are listening for the warnings of apostles and prophets around them, and help their churches prepare for what's ahead. Like my pastor, they are lifeguards who aren't just *watching*, but are also *training* their people to swim! Scriptures include: Titus 1:7-9; 1 Peter 5:2-3; Hebrews 13:17.

Teachers: These are familiar enough with scripture to identify religious deceptions and spot a counterfeit a mile away. **Doctrinally sound teachers use the Bible as their life jacket,** and they long to clothe others in the same truths they have discovered themselves. They know that holding fast to the Word of truth is what saves you. (See 1 Corinthians 15:1-11.) Scriptures include: 1 Timothy 4:16; 6:20; 2 Timothy 4; Titus 2:1; 2 Timothy 2:15.

If you are an "everyday believer" who is not yet functioning as a leader, you have, at the very least, a mandate to be on guard for yourself. (See Luke 21:34; 2 Tim. 2:4.) The best way to do this is to stay attentive to your Divine Lifeguard, Jesus, obeying His commands and listening to His warnings. If you do get in "over your head," He will rescue you! (Psalm 91:15)

On that warm summer day, I was ready to rescue any children at our church on the lake. I am also ready to rescue those who are struggling in their relationship with God.

I hope that spiritually, you are ready, too. Will you rescue the perishing? Will you watch, pray, teach, train, and warn the Body? Will you be a spiritual lifeguard?

I will stand at my guard post and station myself on the lookout tower. I will watch to see what He will say to me and what I should reply about my complaint. –Habbakuk 2:1; HCSB

11
WHAT SOME DESPERATE CHICKENS TAUGHT ME ABOUT DESPERATE PRAYERS

I had the unparalleled joy of running around my yard at 6:48 this morning, half-naked in my robe and slippers, chasing eight mutinous chickens who escaped, somehow, from their coop. I'm sure the neighbors thought I'd lost my mind.

The last time my chickens roamed free, they pooped under said neighbor's bush, which (despite the obvious benefits to the soil) caused an uproar in the town, and required us to seek a variance, since they cannot free-range at will here.

Besides that, it was nearly Easter, and I had no desire to re-mulch the garden beds I'd already tended, if the chickens destroyed them again before my guests arrived.

So there I was, wild-haired and in slippered feet, chasing the hens in the freezing cold and hoping they'd follow me back to their cage. Everyone in the house except the cat had already gone for the day, leaving me alone with no help at all. (Did I mention that the hens escaped because they were desperately hungry? We ran out of chicken feed yesterday, and when I drove to the only feed store in our area, I found a handwritten sign on the door saying that they'd arbitrarily decided to close for the day. Ugh!)

Desperate Times Call for Desperate Measures

I am not a morning person, as anyone in my family will tell you. I don't drink coffee and I wake up slow. So the idea of a "morning run" in the cold, wearing only my robe, does not typically appeal to me.

But time was of the essence. I dared not enrage the neighbors again. So I chased the girls around the yard without success, until I wised up and found a bag of Cheerios someone had given my children (thank you, dear friend - you know who you are!). With this treat I lured most of them to their destination. Slamming the door shut, I breathed an angry sigh of relief.

That was when I noticed that there were only *seven* chickens in the cage, not eight.

Some of you who have been reading my blog for a while might remember Squawky. One of our first "Easter Egger"(Americauna) chickens, she is the redhead of the bunch and - appropriately - the most rebellious. She has escaped us before.

Squawky does not come when called. She runs to the *back* of the coop when you open the door, and the *far* side of the yard when you try to catch her. She is not a compliant chick. And she gave me no end of trouble this morning.

I don't know if you've ever tried to catch a chicken. It isn't easy. Most of them, after they get to know you, will assume a submissive posture when you approach slowly to pick them up, and treat you as the "rooster" if there isn't one in the mix already.

But chickens react adversely to anger, sudden noises, and aggression, all of which I was displaying this morning as I cursed the stupid birds for escaping. I can tell you with certainty that the anger of man does not work the righteousness of God, especially with hens.

So around and around the yard we went, Squawky and I, she clucking and I yelling, all under the watchful eyes of the cat, who was now sitting by the front door I had left open, amused by the whole scene.

I came just close enough to grab Squawky's wings, but she clucked at me and flew away. I set up a barrier to corner her from the other side, and she flew right over it. Finally, she accidentally impaled her head between the holes in the cage and I grabbed her by the feet to capture her.* (*No animals were hurt in the making of this story, I promise!)

By 7:14 AM I was back in my house, huddled by the heater with a cup of tea, trying to calm down.

And then it hit me: *Those chickens were acting just like the enemy!*

Desperate Times Should Call for <u>Prayerful</u> Measures

Like my chickens, Satan sometimes surprises me with untimely harassment that draws me out of my usual place of rest and peace. To hook me, there's almost always an element of urgency to these attacks, and in that moment, I forget to pray.

People say that desperation draws us closer to God, but the truth is, sometimes it doesn't. In my desperation to "fix" a situation, I will jump right into the chaos the enemy creates and accomplish nothing because of my own anger and frustration!

*Desperate times should call for **prayerful** measures, not desperate ones!*

Most of the time, our chickens are a tremendous blessing to us. They give us beautiful, organic eggs and fascinate us with their diverse personalities. But when the enemy messes with that blessing, it is a natural instinct on my part to want to fight to protect what he is trying to steal.

Fighting battles in my own strength is unfruitful, as I was reminded this morning. Had I taken a more submissive posture before God **first** this morning, I might have received a better strategy or kept my peace.

The moral of the story is this: *don't* run around like an oversized chicken in a bathrobe when the enemy shows up. Spiritually, you should soar like an eagle, not run like a chicken! Take a minute to pray a desperate prayer and let God give you a higher strategy. I promise, that prayer will save you a lot of grief... and embarrassment.

"The thief comes only to steal and kill and destroy; I came that they may have life, and have it abundantly."

~John 10:10, NASB

12
DO YOU PRAY THIS POWERFUL PRAYER?

Let me be the first to admit that sometimes, my prayers don't get answered. It happens to everyone. We're all on a journey, growing in the knowledge of who God is and how He works. No one - not even the most "spiritual" believer you know - has his prayers answered all the time!

But in thirty-plus years of growing in the Lord, I've discovered that there are some prayers that are *powerful.* More powerful than others. One such prayer is asking God for what I call "Divine Appointments."

Prayer in the Produce Aisle

I prayed this prayer for "divine appointments" one day on the way to the supermarket. I was heading to a conference for the weekend, and needed to make a quick trip to the store to pick up some food for my family.

On the way, in the car, I prayed: *"Lord, I thank you for your divine appointments today. Put me on YOUR schedule. Rearrange my agenda if need be, so that I do what YOU are doing and bring you glory today. Amen."*

That's it. That was my prayer. I arrived at the store, and had no sooner walked into the produce aisle than I heard someone call my name. "Deborah! *Deborah!* I'm so glad to see you!"

I turned around and saw an acquaintance of mine standing there, waving me over. She is what you might call an *extreme* introvert, spending most of her time inside her house. Despite the fact that she lived nearby, I had not seen this quiet grandmother for several months.

Surprisingly, she was delighted to see me. I know this because for the next 45 minutes - *in the apple section* - she poured out a story of family trauma so heart-wrenching it brought *both* of us to tears. She was at wit's end, and did not know how to repair the breaches her family divisions had caused. There seemed to be no solution.

"Have you prayed?" I asked.

"No... I used to pray a lot, a long time ago, when I was a single mom. I really needed God then," she answered.

"So you already know how to talk to Him," I said.

"Yes, I just don't do it that often."

My neighbor is a non-practicing Catholic who, like many people, reaches out for God more when she's in need. Perhaps because I had been transparent with her over the years concerning my faith, she reached eagerly for me, hoping I could help. Unfortunately, I was no more able to solve her family difficulties than she was - but I knew the One who could!

"It might be a good idea to bring this issue before God in prayer," I suggested. "There seems to be no human way to intervene, but God is not limited. He may have a solution we have not thought of."

I was aware that time was running out; I had a conference to attend and I had not finished my shopping. I knew that my friend was hurting and needed help, and I promised to pray for her.

"In fact," I said hesitantly, "If you'd like, we can pray together right now."

I fully expected a "no" answer. After all, we were standing in the middle of the apple harvest in a grocery store! To my surprise, she readily agreed.

As I prayed for her, tears began streaming down her face. She let me continue, apparently oblivious to the shoppers around us, who probably wondered what could be so terribly wrong with the produce!

By the time I left the supermarket, I was praising God. *A usually-isolated acquaintance had just had a deep and powerful encounter with God. Truly that was a "divine appointment!"*

Power in Your Prayers

I could tell you many stories connected to this one powerful prayer. I pray for divine appointments regularly and have had opportunities to talk with people I never expected to run into during the course of my days. Coincidences? I don't think so. I have bumped into friends, encouraged believers, and even led a stranger to the Lord. One day, because my youngest son begged me for a haircut, I witnessed to an entire group of stylists in a salon!

Praying for "divine appointments" is all about giving up your agenda and getting onto God's schedule. It's a powerful prayer because when we lose our life - our way of doing things - we gain His. We align ourselves with God's purposes. Listen to the words of Jesus: *"I have come down from heaven, not to do My own will, but the will of Him who sent me."* (John 6:38, NKJV). Sometimes we wonder what the will of God is for us, and it's really very simple. John 6:29 spells it out for us: *"This is the work of God, that you* **believe** *in Him whom He sent."*

When we believe in a God who is "working all things together for the good of those who love Him" (Romans 8:28); in a God who is "sustaining all things by the word of His power" (Hebrews 1:3); and who "directs our footsteps" (Proverbs 16:9), we will have no trouble believing that we can do His work on His timetable. We can confidently pray for "divine appointments" and then watch Him put together a schedule so timely, so fulfilling, so powerful and so _fun_ that we cannot help

but worship Him even more!

APPENDICES

I.
"ASK BOLDLY!"

To believe God for greater things requires that we know Him in greater ways. "Asking Boldly" in prayer means that we move beyond superficiality, standing firmly on our relationship with God as Father. God's compassion is stirred by those who attend to him daily, listening for His Word and seeking His face. God is looking for deep friendship with people, and for those friends, He has great promises! Here is a prophetic word the Lord spoke to me during a quiet time concerning His heart towards our prayers.

"The way is open. <u>The Way</u> is open.
The way is <u>**open!**</u>

"I say to you that your Maker has open hands, an open heart, and an open invitation to you to come up higher! Out of the abundance of My love I open My home to you, just as you have opened yours to Me already. Take hold of the benefits of our friendship. Come and visit Me often, for I love your presence as much as you love

Mine. You find that hard to believe, for your sins have stood in your way in the past, but now they are removed, and there is no reason for you to hide yourself any longer!

"Come daily into My Presence, for you will find that the riches of our friendship are more than enough to satisfy your hungry heart, even when others have failed to satisfy you. Take hold of My open hand, step across the threshold of grace I have prepared for you, and enter in to the abundance that comes from a life of relationship with Me.

"For you come empty, but I am full. You come dissatisfied, but your satisfaction can be found in Me. You come feeling lost, wondering even if you have the right address for Me, and yet if you would look up from your wanderings you would see Me standing at the very door, welcoming you. Wisdom calls to her children, and I am calling you up higher, into the mansions of My glory, to discover new things you have not expected to see yet.

"The time has advanced rapidly and you have not noticed it coming, but I tell you, it is here: the time of My GOODNESS is at hand. The time to receive blessings is at hand. The time of renewed relationship is at hand. Look carefully at My hands and see that I hold nothing from you: it is all yours for the taking. 'Ask whatever you will, and it shall be done for you.' (John 15:7.)

"Come boldly into My Presence, for you have need of My help. Allow me to fill the emptiness. Ask Me for the things you want to see happen in the earth at this time, for there will never be another time quite like this. My mercy is at hand. Oh, if My people only knew the depth of My goodness to them, they would RUN to Me in earnest, never doubting!

"You must discard the faulty ways of thinking about Me to take hold of Me in this season. *To retain your fears is to miss My fire.* If you would be a 'burning one,' one filled with My passion, you must discard all that quenches that flame. Be ruthless in your quest to ignite passion for Me, and I will add the wind of My Spirit to your efforts to fan the flame.

"Ask boldly! Make your requests known to Me! You have not because you ask not. You do not ask someone you know only superficially to do great favors for you. To believe Me for greater things means knowing Me in deeper ways. Though a bride and groom are bound in covenant, they may still feel the pain of separation or the lack of intimacy.

"I am looking for the intimacy that has courage to request miracles, to make a demand on My goodness and bring My manifest Presence into the earth, in YOUR sphere of influence. To whom would you introduce Me? What favors would you like Me to perform for those you know who are in need? Realize that as an indwelling Spirit, I see the world through *your* eyes now, and respond to the requests *you* make in prayer for the needs *you* see. I am stirred by your compassion.

"Ask Me to make a way for someone. I will do it because I love you! Work together with Me in your corner of the world. Have confidence that I will join you as you request My Presence to go and meet the needs you see. For you are My dwelling place, and I come and go in the earth through you, as you and I determine together your every step."

© *Deborah Perkins / www.HisInscriptions.com, 2017*

II.

HOW TO PRAY FOR YOUR SPIRITUAL CHILDREN

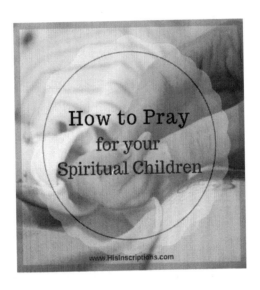

Father, I pray that my spiritual children may abound more and more in all knowledge and spiritual discernment. Let them know Your love deeply, Lord. Let them approve the things that are excellent, being filled with the fruits of righteousness in Christ so that they glorify You. Keep them sincere and without offense until the day of Christ's return. (From Paul's letter to the Philippians)

May all my spiritual children be filled with the knowledge of God's will in all wisdom and spiritual understanding! Help them to walk worthy of you, Lord, pleasing You fully in all things. Give them fruitfulness in every good work they do. Help them to increase in the knowledge of God. Strengthen them with might and divine power, so that they can be patient and endure suffering with joy. Give them a heart of thankfulness to You for the inheritance You have promised them. (Colossians)

Thank you, Father, for these children, who are growing in faith, hope, and love. Give me opportunities to be with them, so that I can supply what is lacking in their faith. When I am absent from them, reassure them that my heart is still with them. (1 Thessalonians)

Give my spiritual children a Spirit of wisdom and revelation in the knowledge of You, Lord. Open the eyes of their understanding, enlightening them so that they know the hope of their calling, the riches of Your glorious inheritance, and the exceeding greatness of Your power towards them as they believe. Strengthen these children with might through Your Holy Spirit in their inner man, so that Christ may dwell in their hearts through faith. I pray that each one will be rooted and grounded in love, and know the extent of Your love that passes beyond all sense-knowledge. Let them be filled with the fullness of God today! (Ephesians)

Father, I pray that those I disciple in the faith would be like-minded towards one another. Fill them with joy and peace as they believe in You, so that they abound in hope. Let all that they do be done in love. May Your grace surround them constantly. (Romans)

When my children encounter suffering, Lord, let them turn to You, the Father of all comfort, who will comfort them in every tribulation so that they in turn can comfort others with the consolations You give them. Let any afflictions in their lives be endured like good soldiers of Christ, with the power given to them at salvation. Remind them of their eternal glory. Thank you that You always lead them in triumph in Christ, diffusing the fragrance of Your knowledge in every place! (2 Corinthians)

Let the grace of the Lord Jesus, and the love of God, and the communion of the Holy Spirit be with each one, Father. In Jesus' Name. Amen.

© *Deborah Perkins / www.HisInscriptions.com*

III.

PRAYERS FOR THE END TIMES

Inspired by 2 Thessalonians

Father, let faith, love and patience grow in all the tribulations, persecutions, and rejections I endure, so that I am counted worthy of the Kingdom of God and bring You glory.

~2 Thessalonians 1:3-5; Matthew 24:13

Deliver me from deception, and protect me from the shaking and troubling of my mind or spirit by the lawless one. Help me to stand fast in the truth, established and secure, comforted by the hope of Your coming.

~2 Thessalonians 1:2; Matthew 24:4

I pray that the written and spoken Word of God will run swiftly and bear fruit in every place that I and others publish Your Good News! Deliver me from unreasonable and wicked men who have no faith; establish me and guard me from the evil one.

~2 Thessalonians 3:1-3

Jesus, keep me from being upset by godless leaders, wars, and rumors of wars. I believe You shorten the end times for the sake of Your people, and I will continue to believe and preach the Gospel until You come.

~2 Thessalonians 2:16-17; Matthew 24:3, 6

Lord, help me to watch for Your coming with patience and hope, having my spiritual life in order and being ready to meet you. If I must flee from tribulation, let my flight be at a time when I am rested and ready, when even the weather itself is advantageous to me.

~2 Thessalonians 1:7-10; Matthew 24:20, 42; Matthew 25:1-13

Holy Spirit, help me to work quietly, live honestly, and serve cheerfully in troubled times.

~2 Thessalonians 3:12-13

Father, please direct my heart into Your love and patience. Give me Your peace at all times and in every way!

~2 Thessalonians 3:5, 16

IV.

TIPS FOR QUALITY TIME WITH JESUS

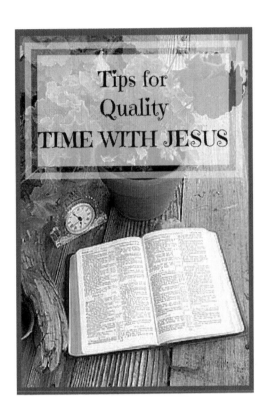

Distractions so easily hinder our devotional times with Jesus! To make your quiet time quality time, it's important to tackle three major areas where the enemy can gain a foothold. Use this checklist of tips to improve your daily prayer times.

1. Silence the World

Find a room with a door you can close to be alone – even the car will work in a pinch!

Turn off cell phones, tablets & TV; silence all electronics and/or notifications.

Remove anything that would distract you: books, to-do list, clutter. You will need:

- Your Bible
- A Notebook & Pen
- Bible Study or Devotional
- Anything else essential to your communication with God, such as a musical instrument or painting/sketching supplies.

Scriptures: Matthew 6:5-6; Psalm 150

2. Silence the Flesh

Keep a small pad of paper handy, near your Bible. If you remember something that you must do today or don't want to forget, simply write it down and set it aside for later.

Sit, stand, or relax comfortably. Your body's posture doesn't matter; what's important is that discomfort does not distract you from keeping the posture of your heart at peace!

If you need water (or coffee, if it's early!), make sure you prepare a cup ahead of time to avoid interrupting your conversation with God. Ditto for trips to the bathroom!

Ask family members (if at home) to leave you undisturbed while you are in your quiet time, except for emergencies. Small children, of course, cannot be left unsupervised, but an elementary or tween-age child can be taught what constitutes an "emergency" and given something to occupy themselves for a short time while you pray. Parents should never feel guilty for taking time out for themselves! It teaches our children respect for God and authority, sets a positive example for their own spiritual lives, and refreshes us for the rest of our day with them. If your children cannot be left alone, pray before they wake, or teach them to pray alongside you, with their own small Bibles or coloring pages, so that they develop this healthy, lifelong habit.

3. Silence the Devil

There are two things in particular that the devil likes to use to sever our connection with God. The first is **sin**, the second is **condemnation**.

To deal with sin - Take a few moments at the beginning of your time with God to **ask the Holy Spirit if there is any sin that needs to be confessed.** Most common are sins of anger, offense, and unforgiveness. Listen quietly to your heart, and if He shows you something, acknowledge the sin and repent before moving on. If your conscience is clear, you will know that any accusations the devil brings up later are unfounded.

*A subset of sin is the group of smaller, "besetting sins" that take time for us to overcome, such as worry, fear, or anxiety. Grief, loss, and sickness may also linger here. These "little foxes" can spoil our time in the beautiful garden of God's Presence. When problems like these interrupt your quiet time, take a moment to bind them in the Name of Jesus and forbid them from distracting you. Speak your command out loud and do as David did: still and quiet your soul (Psalm 131:2).

Scriptures: 1 John 1:9; Ephesians 1:7; Acts 24:16; Matthew 5:23-24; Matthew 18:18

To dismiss condemnation – As you are talking with God or interacting with His Word, the devil may remind you of ways that you haven't "measured up" recently, or failures along the way. If there is unconfessed sin, then acknowledge it and move on, as above. **A nagging sense of unworthiness is condemnation from the devil, not true conviction of the Holy Spirit.** We are all "in process," as children of God growing to maturity, and mistakes are allowed in the framework of His grace and great love for us! Remember, **conviction's goal is restoration and relationship. Condemnation's goal is separation and self-hatred.**

Scriptures: 1 Timothy 1:5; Hebrews 10:22; Romans 8:33-39.

4. **Enter in!**

Hebrews 4:16 says: "Let us therefore come boldly to the throne of grace, that we may obtain mercy and find grace to help in time of need." There is no "right way" to approach God in this New Testament time of grace. Like a loving father, God is always ready to embrace you and welcome you into His Presence. Some of us run into His arms, others come awkwardly, timidly or respectfully. He loves and understands each one of us!

When we hide behind religious rituals or legalistic interpretations of how we should pray, we unwittingly close off our hearts to honest and free interactions with Him. Patterns for prayer, such as the ACTS acronym (Adoration, confession, thanksgiving, supplication), the Lord's Prayer, or praying through the Old Testament Tabernacle can be helpful, but they are meant only to direct us to the real thing: ***personal* communication with a loving Father.**

Are you tired? Tell Him about it! Thankful? Praise Him! Concerned for someone? Pray prayers of supplication. Start where you are, because once you have unburdened your own heart it is easier to hear from His. Ask Him to give you understanding of His Word as you read. **Share what's on your heart, and expect Him to share what's on His in return. That's relationship!**

Many Christians enjoy using worship music to enter in to God's presence, in conjunction with prayer. God inhabits our praises (Psalm 22:3) and He shows up when we pray (James 4:8). Worship and/or pray, inviting Him into your quiet time.

Scriptures: *Ephesians 3:12; Hebrews 10:19-22; Acts 4:31; Luke 24:45; Matthew 6:7*

5. **Listen**.

Quality time in relationships includes listening, not just speaking. Once you feel you have entered into a place of God's peace and presence, take some time to read the Word and record your thoughts about what He is saying to you. How can you do this?

- **Journal** your thoughts as they come to you
- **Copy** down Bible verses that seem to jump off the page
- **Memorize** a scripture that is especially meaningful to you that day
- **Write** a song or a poem based on the theme of your conversation with God
- **Color**, sketch, or paint a picture of what He is showing you, or of a story you read in the Bible.
- Is God asking you to **act** on a specific command? Think about how you might put His Word into action today.
- **Meditate** on a significant passage. Put yourself in the context of the story. What would it feel like to be the woman at the well? Jesus? An onlooker? A disciple? A villager? Record your thoughts.
- **Share** (in a note, an email or on social media) something encouraging the Lord is

saying to you, with a friend. Use your time with God as a jumping-off point for prophetic encouragement and service to others.

- Finally, **Pray** the scriptures back to God. Use the verses you have just read to pray for yourself and others in the Body of Christ. (See 1 Timothy 2:1-4.) Make the verse personal: for example, when you read 2 Corinthians 5:21 ("For He made Him who knew no sin to be sin for us, that we might become the righteousness of God in Him,") say, "I am the righteousness of God in Christ! I pray that my children will also become righteous by accepting Christ's sacrifice for themselves!"

Above all, be sensitive to what the Holy Spirit leads you to do in your quiet times. Just as our human interactions are rarely the same from day to day, so our relationship with God will thrive on variety and change. Let the Holy Spirit lead you; some days might be full of worship, others may be dedicated to intercessory prayer. I have had extended times of study in the Word that seemed like a supernatural "feast!" In all things, be free to enjoy your relationship with Jesus as He reveals more and more of Himself to you. This is the secret to quality time!

© *Deborah Perkins / HisInscriptions.com. All Scripture References NKJV.*

ABOUT THE AUTHOR

Author and speaker **Deborah Perkins** has over 30 years of Christian leadership experience across denominations. She inspires people worldwide to **"Discover Life-Giving Communication with God."** Her first Bible Study, <u>**How to Inherit Your Spiritual Promises: 5 Steps to Success**</u> was published in 2016.

At God's request in 2014, she founded **His Inscriptions**, a non-profit, 501c3 ministry whose online audience now numbers in the thousands. Chapters in this book first appeared on the blog at His Inscriptions, where Deborah encourages her readers weekly. To learn more, or to sow a gift into this ministry, please visit **www.HisInscriptions.com**.

Follow Deborah and His Inscriptions on <u>Facebook</u>, <u>YouTube</u>, <u>Twitter</u>, and <u>Pinterest</u> daily. Like this book? Leave a review on Amazon!

"Behold, I have inscribed you on the palms of My hands; your walls are continually before Me."
~Isaiah 49:16; Holy Bible, NASB

62536318R00062

Made in the USA
Middletown, DE
23 January 2018